Written and edited by David Fentiman
Editor Anant Sagar
Art Editor Radhika Banerjee
Assistant Art Editor Pallavi Kapur
Managing Editors Laura Gilbert,
Chitra Subramanyam
Managing Art Editors Maxine Pedliham,
Neha Ahuja
Art Director Lisa Lanzarini
DTP Designer Umesh Singh Rawat
Pre-Production Producer Marc Staples
Pre-Production Manager Sunil Sharma
Producer Alex Bell
Reading Consultant Linda B. Gambrell, Ph.D

Publisher Julie Ferris
Publishing Director Simon Beecroft

For Lucasfilm
Executive Editor Jonathan W. Rinzler
Art Director Troy Alders
Story Group Rayne Roberts, Pablo Hidalgo, Leland Chee

First published in the United States in 2015 by DK Publishing
345 Hudson Street, New York, New York 10014

Page design copyright © 2015 Dorling Kindersley Limited
A Penguin Random House Company
10 9 8 7 6 5 4 3 2 1
001–259627–Jan/2015

A CIP catalog record for this book
is available from the Library of Congress.

ISBN: 978-1-4654-1988-0 (Hardback)
ISBN: 978-1-4654-1989-7 (Paperback)

Color Reproduction by Altaimage Ltd, UK
Printed and bound in China by South China Printing Company Ltd.

www.starwars.com
www.dk.com

A WORLD OF IDEAS:
SEE ALL THERE IS TO KNOW

FIGHT THE
EMPIRE

Written by David Fentiman

Contents

The Empire's Rule

Many years ago, the evil Empire took over the galaxy, replacing the Republic government. The Republic tried to be fair and noble, but the Empire is harsh and cruel. Many worlds were taken over by the Empire's army. One of these worlds was the peaceful planet of Lothal.

Since then, the Empire has ruled Lothal. The Empire's brutal soldiers, known as stormtroopers, stand watch over everything. There is little freedom. Life on Lothal is very tough.

Fighting Back

The Empire is very strong, and has powerful weapons and vehicles. Some people do not accept the Empire's rule, and fight back against it in any way they can. These fighters will come to be known as rebels.

A small crew of rebels works together to battle the Empire on Lothal. The rebels' names are Kanan, Ezra, Hera, Zeb, Sabine, and Chopper. They all have different skills and abilities, but they fight against the Empire together.

LOTHAL

The Voice of the Empire on Lothal

New security rules

Strict Imperial laws will make Lothal secure.

BREAKING NEWS

REBEL ATTACK!

DAMAGE STATS

3 TIE FIGHTERS **DESTROYED!**

7 IMPERIAL SOLDIERS **INJURED!**

9 WEAPON CRATES **STOLEN!**

The rebel criminals have struck again. Imperial TIE fighters docked in Capital City were attacked and destroyed using powerful explosives. This is the third rebel attack in the last two weeks.

An Imperial official told the *Bulletin*, "We are creating new, stronger defenses to protect us from the rebel threat. Anyone who is found helping these rebels will be arrested and punished."

BULLETIN

Edition XVII Volume II

Find the rebels

The Empire has promised
to capture the criminals.

TIE fighter exploding in Capital City

The Master Planner

Kanan is the leader of the rebel crew. He is a Jedi. The Jedi are guardians who once protected the Republic, but they were nearly all wiped out by the Empire.

Kanan plans the rebels' missions, and leads them into battle. He gives them orders and guides them through trouble.

His Jedi powers, battle tactics, and skill with a lightsaber make Kanan a strong warrior and a brave leader.

Kanan has been fighting the Empire for many years, and the other rebels look up to him.

The Escape Artist

Ezra grew up alone on the streets of Lothal. Over the years he has learned some useful skills to fight the Empire and protect himself.

Ezra knows how to spot the Empire's weaknesses and take advantage of

them. He has been stealing from the Empire for years, but now he does it for the rebels, not just for himself.

Ezra has also learned how to avoid getting caught. He can slip past stormtroopers without being noticed, and even escape from a locked prison cell!

The Ace Pilot

Imperial pilots shouldn't mess with Hera! Her ship, known as the *Ghost*, is bigger than Imperial starfighters, but she flies it like a quick, nimble fighter craft.

She is an ace pilot and knows many tricks to avoid Imperial ships in dogfights. Hera is also an expert with the *Ghost*'s cannons. She has shot down more Imperials than she can count.

When the rebels are in trouble, Hera can fly the *Ghost* through super-tight spots, and outrun or outfly almost any other ship!

Ezra's Diary

I have had an amazing day!
When I tried to steal some Imperial
weapon crates, I got caught up in a
speeder bike chase.

These are my crates. Mine, mine, MINE!

The leader of the group

Very valuable weapons

This guy stinks!

To escape, I ended up jumping into
a starship with a bunch of strangers!
They were trying to steal the crates, too.

It turns out they are rebels
fighting against the Empire.

What's her story?

Ship's pilot

I hate the Empire, too.
Fighting against it sounds
really dangerous, but the
rebels are trying to protect
the people of Lothal.

I've decided I should join them.

The Mechanical Marvel

Chopper is Hera's copilot. He is a type of robot called an astromech droid, but unlike most robots, he is cranky and stubborn.

The rebels would never admit it, but they would be lost without Chopper. He repairs the *Ghost* when it is damaged, and when the rebels go into battle he joins them on their missions.

Chopper can break into Imperial computers to turn off security systems, or send false messages as a decoy. He has even been used as a spy!

The Warrior

Zeb is the closest thing the rebels have to a trained soldier. He served in the army on his homeworld of Lasan, before the Empire invaded it.

Zeb's training makes him a powerful fighter. He can take on whole squads of stormtroopers at once.

His powerful bo-rifle lets him destroy targets at long range, or wade in to fight Imperial soldiers up close.

Zeb's only weakness is that he does not always follow orders. This can put the other rebels in danger.

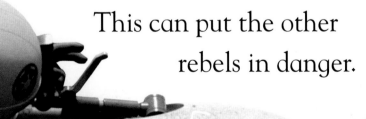

The Explosives Expert

Sabine comes from Mandalore, a planet famous for its warriors. She may be young, but she makes up for it with her bravery and skill.

Sabine is the crew's technology expert. She is a genius with all kinds of gadgets and weapons, and she looks after the rebels' equipment for them.

Sabine's weapons of choice are explosives. She can use them to destroy a single speeder without damaging anything else—or she can blow apart an entire starship!

WARNING!
System hacked by rebels.

Message received

FIGHT THE EMPIRE!

Good people of Lothal,
do not believe what the
Empire tells you.

Sender unknown close

Message received

We are on your side.
We remember Lothal before
the Empire came here.
People could do and say
what they liked, without fear.
We want to free Lothal
from the Empire.

 close

Help us free Lothal!

- Do not help Imperial stormtroopers.

- Give aid to those in need.

- Ignore Imperial messages.

- DO NOT LOSE HOPE!

Sender unknown

close

LONG LIVE THE REBELLION!

Sender unknown

Fighting the Rebel Menace

When the rebels start causing problems for the Empire on Lothal, the Imperials call for reinforcements.

Agent Kallus works for the Empire's secret police. He is trained to hunt rebels down, and then destroy them. Kallus is a powerful warrior, but he is still no match for a Jedi like Kanan.

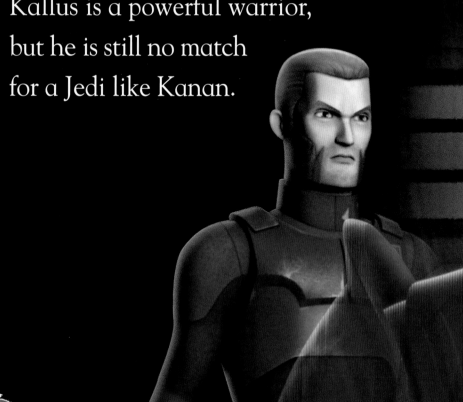

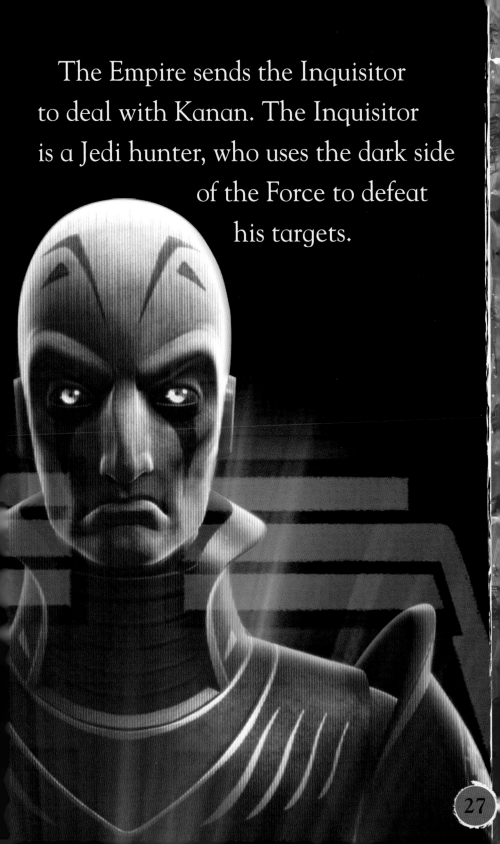

The Empire sends the Inquisitor to deal with Kanan. The Inquisitor is a Jedi hunter, who uses the dark side of the Force to defeat his targets.

Good or Bad?

In the fight for the galaxy, the rebels are on one side, and the Empire is on the other. But there are some in the middle, too.

Some people are simply citizens trying to mind their own business and stay out of the Empire's way.

Others, like Cikatro Vizago, say that business is all that matters. He will help the rebels for the right amount of money—but if the Empire gives him a better offer, then the rebels could be in trouble.

Crooked Officials

The Imperials on Lothal are led by two cruel officials named Taskmaster Grint and Commandant Aresko. They have no respect for the planet's citizens, and call them "Loth-rats." For the Imperials, Lothal exists only to serve the mighty Empire.

Grint and Aresko prefer picking on those who are too weak to fight back. The rebels have fought against them many times. Luckily, the two officials are not the Empire's finest soldiers, and they are easily outsmarted!

Vehicles of the Empire

The Empire has many powerful and dangerous vehicles that it uses to defeat its enemies. Some of these vehicles are light and agile, while others are strong enough to destroy entire cities.

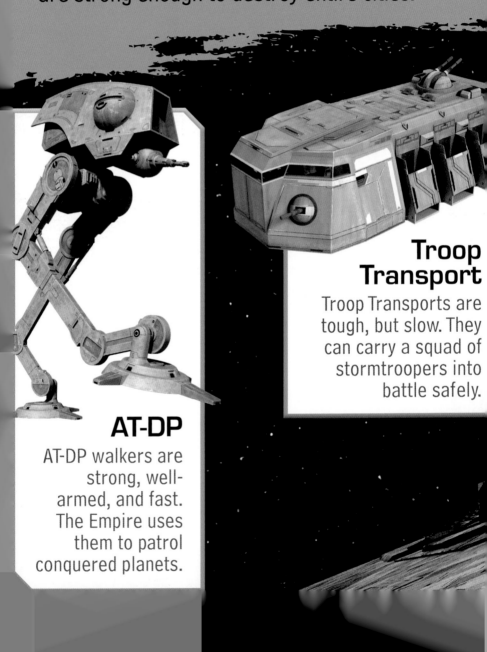

Troop Transport

Troop Transports are tough, but slow. They can carry a squad of stormtroopers into battle safely.

AT-DP

AT-DP walkers are strong, well-armed, and fast. The Empire uses them to patrol conquered planets.

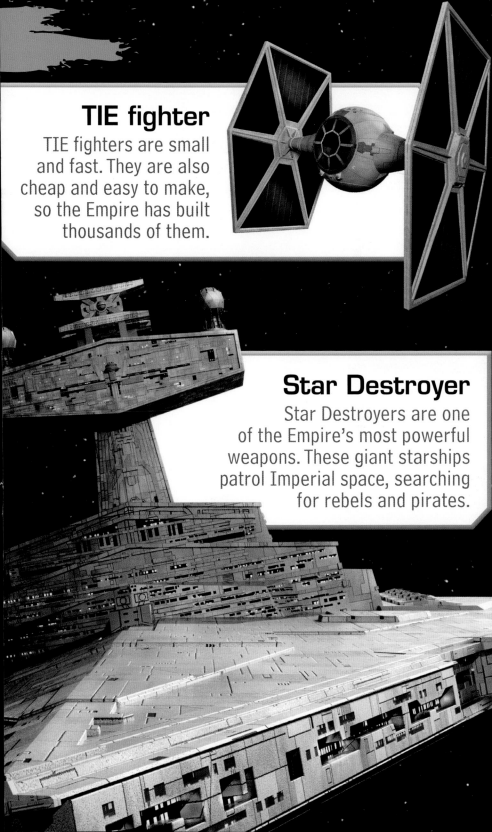

TIE fighter

TIE fighters are small and fast. They are also cheap and easy to make, so the Empire has built thousands of them.

Star Destroyer

Star Destroyers are one of the Empire's most powerful weapons. These giant starships patrol Imperial space, searching for rebels and pirates.

Quick Thinking

Outsmarting the Empire is what the rebels do best. If they are in a tricky situation, the rebels improvise!

When the rebels get trapped on an Imperial freighter with lots of stormtroopers, Chopper turns off the ship's gravity to distract the Imperials.

Another time, the rebels are trapped in a Star Destroyer's hangar. They are surrounded by Agent Kallus and his stormtroopers. Sabine uses explosives to make a hole in the ship. The Imperials are sucked out into space. In the commotion, the rebels make a getaway.

PLANNING A MISSION

Let me sneak in through an air vent—I've done it hundreds of times. The Empire will never even know we were here!

—EZRA

I think we should use my explosives to blast our way in. It's definitely the safest option.

—SABINE

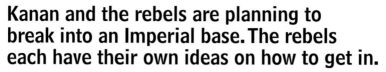

Kanan and the rebels are planning to break into an Imperial base. The rebels each have their own ideas on how to get in.

We should just knock on the door. When it opens I'll pound those stormtroopers with my fists! Problem solved.

—ZEB

I can fly the *Ghost* to land us right inside the base. It'll be really fast.

—HERA

Trapped!

Things do not always go well for the rebels. Agent Kallus has been hunting rebels for a long time, and he has a few tricks of his own.

Kallus knows the rebels will always try to rescue one of their crew, so he captures Ezra to trap the rebels. Sure enough, the rebels arrive on Kallus's Star Destroyer to free Ezra.

But Kallus has underestimated them. Ezra escapes from his cell, and the other rebels blast through Kallus's squad of stormtroopers to escape.

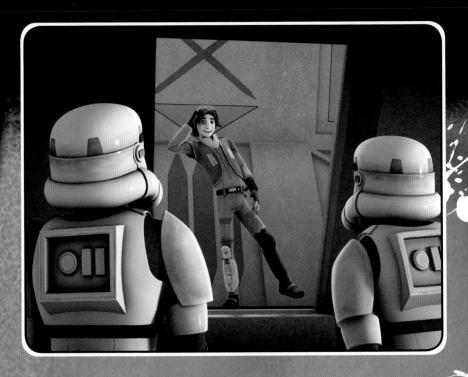

Rebel Raids

Stealing from the Empire is one of the rebels' most important missions.

The Empire has become lazy, and does not guard its cargo shipments very well. The rebels can swoop in and take what they need before the Empire can react.

Crates of food can be given to the needy. Any stolen weapons can be used against the Empire, or sold for valuable credits. The rebels need credits to keep food in their bellies and fuel in the *Ghost*!

Rescue Missions

The Empire arrests anyone who dares to speak out against it. They are called traitors and get thrown into prison, or worse.

The rebels must free these prisoners if they can. However, the Empire guards its prisoners well.

A tribe of Wookiees is being held on a mining planet called Kessel. The Empire is using them as slaves. The Wookiees are a strong species, but they will not survive unless they are rescued.

SAVING THE

1

The rebels use their different skills to help free the Wookiees.

2

Ezra leaps into action and uses his tools to unlock the Wookiees' shackles.

3

He uses his Jedi powers to hold off the Imperial soldiers and Agent Kallus.

Kanan turns on his lightsaber.

WOOKIEES!

4

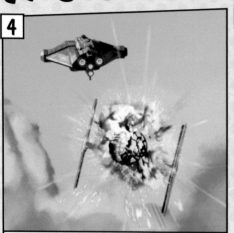

Hera uses the *Ghost* to shoot down Imperial TIE fighters.

5

Zeb and Sabine shoot at the stormtroopers. Then they lead the Wookiees to the *Ghost*.

6

Hera and Sabine pick up the Wookiees and take them to safety.

7

By working together, the rebels have rescued the Wookiees!

Fighting the Jedi Way

The Empire isn't afraid of much, but it is afraid of the Jedi. These brave warriors were strong enough to stand up to the Empire. The Jedi used their powers to defend people from evil, so the Imperials tried to destroy them all.

Kanan hid away for a long time, but now he will use his Jedi skills to fight the Empire. His lightsaber can deflect blaster fire, and cut through almost anything. His Force powers can knock over enemies, or throw people to safety.

Jedi Hunter

The evil Imperial Inquisitor has only one mission: to hunt down Jedi. He uses the dark side of the Force to search for them. When he finds a Jedi, he can instantly sense their strengths and weaknesses. His advanced fighting skills and double-bladed lightsaber make him very dangerous.

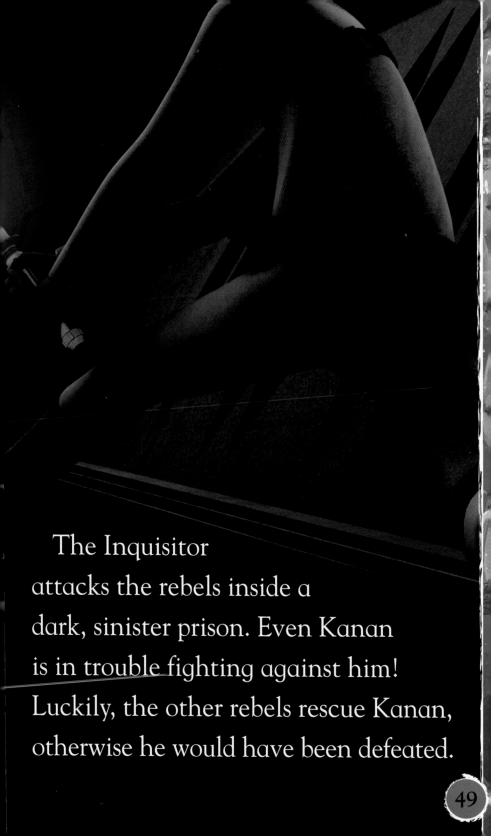

The Inquisitor
attacks the rebels inside a
dark, sinister prison. Even Kanan
is in trouble fighting against him!
Luckily, the other rebels rescue Kanan,
otherwise he would have been defeated.

HOW TO SPOT A JEDI!

BRAVE SOLDIERS OF THE EMPIRE, THE JEDI ARE OUR ENEMIES!

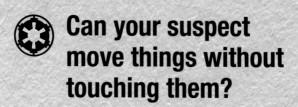 Can your suspect move things without touching them?

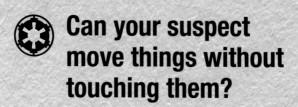 Do they often close their eyes while concentrating?

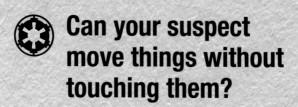 Do they know what is going to happen before it does?

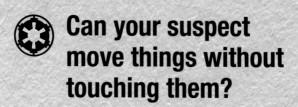 Do they talk about something called "the Force"?

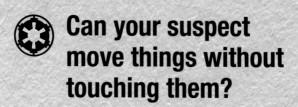 Do they carry a lightsaber?

 IF THE ANSWER TO ANY OF THESE QUESTIONS IS **YES** RAISE THE ALARM IMMEDIATELY!

Flying High

The rebels are always looking for new ways to disrupt the Empire's rule and annoy the Imperials.

Zeb and Erza are on the run from some stormtroopers when they spot a parked TIE fighter. The two rebels steal the TIE and make their escape!

The arrogant Imperials never expect the rebels to do such daring things.

The brave rebels must use all of their skills and abilities to defeat the Empire. They will not stop fighting until Lothal is free!

Situation

Imperial TIE fighters attack the *Ghost*.

• • Plan of attack • •

1 Kanan uses the ship's guns to shoot down one of the TIE fighters.

2 Chopper fixes the ship's shields and then shoots down another TIE fighter.

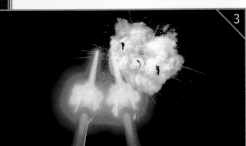

3 Hera's tactical flying skills help the rebels escape from the Empire.

Result: Rebel Victory!

Situation

Agent Kallus has captured Ezra!

• • Plan of attack • •

1 The rebels use the *Ghost* to break into Kallus's Star Destroyer.

2 Ezra escapes from his cell by fooling his guards. He meets the rebels in the hangar.

3 Sabine creates a diversion using powerful explosives. The rebels make their escape!

Result: Rebel Victory!

Fighting the Inquisito

Situation

Kanan battles the Inquisitor using his Jedi skills.

• • Plan of attack • •

1 The Inquisitor is too strong. He can predict all of Kanan's lightsaber attacks!

2 The Inquisitor uses the Force to throw Kanan into a wall, knocking him out.

3 Ezra distracts the Inquisitor using his slingshot. He helps Kanan to make a quick getaway!

Result: Draw

Saving the Farmers

Situation

The Empire arrests Lothal farmers and burns down their farms.

• • Plan of attack • •

1 Ezra jumps onto the transport that is carrying the Empire's prisoners.

2 Using a stolen TIE fighter, Zeb gives him cover fire. Ezra fights off the stormtroopers.

3 Ezra unlocks the doors and frees the farmers from the stormtroopers!

Result: Rebel Victory!

Quiz

1. Who did the Empire replace when it took over the galaxy?

2. Who has shot down more Imperials than she can count?

3. What kind of droid is Chopper?

4. What weapon does Zeb use?

5. What planet is Sabine from?

6. Who thinks that business is all that matters?

7. Where are the Wookiees being held?

8. What are the giant starships of the Empire known as?

9. Who attacks the rebels in a dark, sinister prison?

10. What did Zeb and Ezra steal?

Answers
on page 61

Glossary

Commotion
Noisy excitement
and confusion.

Conquer
To take control
of something by
using force.

Diversion
To take attention
away from
something.

Dogfight
A battle between
aircraft or
starships.

Empire
A group of worlds
or nations ruled
by an Emperor.

Hack
To secretly get
access to files
on a computer.

Improvise
To do something
without planning.

Rebel
Someone who
does not follow
the rules.

Reinforcements
Things that are
sent to help an
army or person.

Tactics
The skill of
organizing
equipment and
soldiers in battle.

Index

Answers to the quiz on pages 58 and 59:
1. The Republic 2. Hera 3. Astromech 4. Bo-rifle
5. Mandalore 6. Cikatro Vizago 7. Kessel
8. Star Destroyers 9. The Inquisitor 10. A TIE fighter

Guide for Parents

DK Readers is a four-level interactive reading adventure series for children, developing the habit of reading widely for both pleasure and information. These books have an exciting main narrative interspersed with a range of reading genres to suit your child's reading ability, as required by the Common Core State Standards. Each book is designed to develop your child's reading skills, fluency, grammar awareness, and comprehension in order to build confidence and engagement when reading.

Ready for a *Reading Alone* book

YOUR CHILD SHOULD

- be able to read most words without needing to stop and break them down into sound parts.
- read smoothly, in phrases and with expression. By this level, your child will be mostly reading silently.
- self-correct when some word or sentence doesn't sound right.

A Valuable and Shared Reading Experience

For some children, text reading, particularly non-fiction, requires much effort, but adult participation can make this both fun and easier. So here are a few tips on how to use this book with your child.

TIP 1 Check out the contents together before your child begins:

- invite your child to check the blurb, contents page, and layout of the book and comment on it.
- ask your child to make predictions about the story.
- talk about the information your child might want to find out.

TIP 2 Encourage fluent and flexible reading:

- support your child to read in fluent, expressive phrases, making full use of punctuation and thinking about the meaning.

- encourage your child to slow down and check information where appropriate.

TIP 3 Indicators that your child is reading for meaning:

- your child will be responding to the text if he/she is self-correcting and varying his/her voice.
- your child will want to talk about what he/she is reading or is eager to turn the page to find out what will happen next.

TIP 4 Share and discuss:

- encourage your child to recall specific details after each chapter.
- provide opportunities for your child to pick out interesting words and discuss what they mean.
- discuss how the author captures the reader's interest, or how effective the non-fiction layouts are.
- ask questions about the text. These help to develop comprehension skills and awareness of the language used.

A FEW ADDITIONAL TIPS

- Read to your child regularly to demonstrate fluency, phrasing, and expression; to find out or check information; and for sharing enjoyment.
- Encourage your child to reread favorite texts to increase reading confidence and fluency.
- Check that your child is reading a range of different types of material, such as poems, jokes, and following instructions.

Series consultant, **Dr. Linda Gambrell**, Distinguished Professor of Education at Clemson University, has served as President of the National Reading Conference, the College Reading Association, and the International Reading Association. She is also reading consultant for the **DK Adventures**.

Have you read these other great books from DK?

Meet the heroes of Chima™ and help them find the Legend Beasts.

Meet the sharks who live on the reef or come passing through.

Can Luke Skywalker help the rebels defeat the evil Empire?

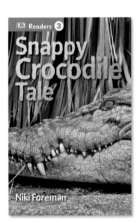

Learn all about Yoda's battles and how he uses the Force.

Follow Chris Croc's adventures from a baby to a mighty king.

Join David on an amazing trip to meet elephants in Asia and Africa.